# VEGETARIAN MAIN MEALS

## · Cooking for Today ·

# VEGETARIAN MAIN MEALS

KATHRYN HAWKINS

||| · PARRAGON · |||

First published in Great Britain in 1996 by
Parragon Book Service Ltd
Unit 13–17
Avonbridge Trading Estate
Atlantic Road
Avonmouth
Bristol BS11 9QD

ISBN 0-7525-1804-6

Produced by Haldane Mason, London

Printed in Italy


*Acknowledgements:*
*Art Direction:* Ron Samuels
*Editor:* Vicky Hanson
*Series Design:* Pedro & Frances Prá-Lopez/Kingfisher Design, London
*Page Design:* Somewhere Creative
*Photography & Styling:* Patrick McLeavey
*Home Economist:* Kathryn Hawkins

Photographs on pages 6, 34, 48, 62 reproduced by permission of ZEFA Picture Library (UK) Ltd.
Photograph on page 20 reproduced by permission of Vicky Hanson.

***Note:***
Cup measurements in this book are for American cups. Tablespoons are assumed to be 15 ml.
Unless otherwise stated, milk is assumed to be full-fat, eggs are standard size 2
and pepper is freshly ground black pepper.

# Contents

# CHAPTER ONE

# *Vegetable Dishes*

Vegetables are at the very heart of a balanced vegetarian diet. They come in many shapes, sizes, colours, flavours and textures. A shopping trolley full of vegetables is going to be cheaper than one packed with meat and fish, so it can be more economical to be a vegetarian as well as being good for your health. Crisp, refreshing vegetables can help cleanse the body's digestive system and maintain the perfect working balance.

Don't just serve vegetables as accompaniments, make a meal of them: Coconut Vegetable Curry (see page 18) is packed full of cauliflower, okra, potato and aubergine (eggplant), and Root Croustades with Sunshine (Bell) Peppers (see page 8) is a combination of carrots, potato, celeriac (celery root) and (bell) peppers.

Opposite: *There is such a large variety of fresh vegetables available today, a vegetarian diet need never be dull.*

# ROOT CROUSTADES WITH SUNSHINE (BELL) PEPPERS

*This colourful combination of grated root vegetables and mixed (bell) peppers would make a stunning impression on dinner party guests.*

STEP 3

STEP 4

STEP 5

STEP 6

SERVES 4

1 orange (bell) pepper
1 red (bell) pepper
1 yellow (bell) pepper
3 tbsp olive oil
2 tbsp red wine vinegar
1 tsp French mustard
1 tsp clear honey
salt and pepper
sprigs of fresh flat-leaf parsley to garnish
green vegetables to serve

CROUSTADES:
250 g/8 oz potatoes, grated coarsely
250 g/8 oz carrots, grated coarsely
350 g/12 oz celeriac (celery root), grated coarsely
1 garlic clove, crushed
1 tbsp lemon juice
30 g/1 oz/2 tbsp butter or margarine, melted
1 egg, beaten
1 tbsp vegetable oil

**1** Place the (bell) peppers on a baking sheet and bake in a preheated oven at 190°C/375°F/Gas Mark 5 for 35 minutes, turning after 20 minutes.

**2** Cover with a tea towel (dish cloth) and leave to cool for 10 minutes.

**3** Peel the skin from the cooked (bell) peppers; cut in half and discard the seeds. Thinly slice the flesh into strips and place in a shallow dish.

**4** Put the oil, vinegar, mustard, honey and seasoning in a small screw-top jar and shake well to mix. Pour over the (bell) pepper strips, mix well and leave to marinate for 2 hours.

**5** To make the croustades, put the potatoes, carrots and celeriac (celery root) in a mixing bowl and toss in the garlic and lemon juice.

**6** Mix in the melted butter or margarine and the egg. Season well. Divide the mixture into 8 and pile on to 2 baking sheets lined with baking parchment, forming each into a 10 cm/4 inch round. Brush with oil.

**7** Bake in a preheated oven at 220°C/425°F/Gas Mark 7 for 30–35 minutes until crisp around the edge and golden. Carefully transfer to a warmed serving dish. Heat the (bell) peppers and marinade for 2–3 minutes until warmed through. Spoon the (bell) peppers over the croustades, garnish with parsley and serve with green vegetables.

STEP 1

STEP 2

STEP 5

STEP 6

# SPINACH ROULADE

*A delicious savoury roll, stuffed with Mozzarella cheese and broccoli. Serve as a main course or as an appetizer, in which case it would easily serve six people.*

SERVES 4–6

*500 g/1 lb small spinach leaves*
*2 tbsp water*
*4 eggs, separated*
*1/2 tsp ground nutmeg*
*salt and pepper*
*300 ml/1/2 pint/1 1/4 cups sugocasa (see below) to serve*

FILLING:
*175 g/6 oz small broccoli florets*
*30 g/1 oz/1/4 cup freshly grated Parmesan cheese*
*175 g/6 oz/1 1/2 cups grated Mozzarella cheese*

**1** Wash the spinach and pack, still wet, into a large saucepan. Add the water. Cover with a tight-fitting lid and cook over a high heat for 4–5 minutes until reduced and soft. Drain thoroughly, squeezing out excess water. Chop finely and pat dry with paper towels.

**2** Mix the spinach with the egg yolks, seasoning and nutmeg. Whisk the egg whites until very frothy but not too stiff, and fold into the spinach mixture.

**3** Grease and line a 32 x 23 cm/13 x 9 inch Swiss roll tin. Spread the mixture in the tin and smooth the top. Bake in a preheated oven at 220°C/425°F/Gas Mark 7 for 12–15 minutes until firm and golden.

**4** Meanwhile, cook the broccoli in boiling water for 4–5 minutes until just tender. Drain and keep warm.

**5** Sprinkle a sheet of baking parchment with Parmesan. Turn the cooked base on to the paper and peel away the lining paper. Sprinkle the base with Mozzarella and top with broccoli.

**6** Hold one end of the paper and carefully roll up the spinach base like a Swiss roll. Heat the sugocasa and spoon on to 4 warmed serving plates. Slice the roulade and place on top of the sugocasa.

### SUGOCASA

Sugocasa is a tomato base for sauces. It usually contains pulped tomatoes, sugar, seasoning and onion. If unavailable, use passata (sieved tomatoes), creamed tomatoes or canned chopped tomatoes; these will all require extra seasoning.

**STEP 1**

**STEP 2**

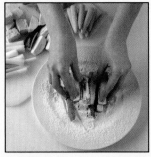

**STEP 4**

**STEP 5**

# TEMPURA-STYLE TOFU (BEAN CURD) & VEGETABLES

*Crispy coated vegetables and tofu (bean curd) accompanied by a sweet, spicy dip give a real taste of the Orient in this Japanese-style dish.*

SERVES 4

*125 g/4 oz baby courgettes (zucchini)*
*125 g/4 oz baby carrots*
*125 g/4 oz baby sweetcorn*
*125 g/4 oz baby leeks*
*2 baby aubergines (eggplant)*
*250 g/8 oz tofu (bean curd)*
*vegetable oil for deep-frying*
*julienne strips of carrot, ginger root and*
*  baby leek to garnish*
*noodles to serve*

*BATTER:*
*2 egg yolks*
*300 ml/$\frac{1}{2}$ pint/1$\frac{1}{4}$ cups water*
*250 g/8 oz/2 cups plain (all-purpose) flour*

*DIPPING SAUCE:*
*5 tbsp mirin or dry sherry*
*5 tbsp Japanese soy sauce*
*2 tsp clear honey*
*1 garlic clove, crushed*
*1 tsp grated ginger root*

**1** Slice the courgettes (zucchini) and carrots in half lengthwise. Trim the baby sweetcorn. Trim the leeks at both ends. Quarter the aubergines (eggplant).

**2** Cut the tofu (bean curd) into 2.5 cm/1 inch cubes.

**3** To make the batter, mix the egg yolks with the water. Sift in 175 g/ 6 oz/1$\frac{1}{2}$ cups of the flour and beat with a balloon whisk to form a thick batter. Don't worry if there are any lumps. Heat the oil for deep-frying to 190°C/375°F or until a cube of bread browns in 30 seconds.

**4** Place the remaining flour on a large plate and toss the vegetables and tofu (bean curd) until lightly coated.

**5** Dip the tofu (bean curd) in the batter and deep-fry for 2–3 minutes until lightly golden. Drain on paper towels and keep warm.

**6** Dip the vegetables in the batter and deep-fry a few at a time for 3–4 minutes until golden. Drain and place on a warmed serving plate.

**7** To make the dipping sauce, mix all the ingredients together. Serve with the vegetables and tofu (bean curd), accompanied with noodles and garnished with julienne strips of vegetables.

# POTATO GNOCCHI WITH GARLIC & HERB SAUCE

*These little potato dumplings are a traditional Italian appetizer but, served with a salad and bread, they make a substantial meal. If you want to serve them as an appetizer, they would serve six people.*

SERVES 4–6

*1 kg/2 lb old potatoes, cut into 1 cm/½ inch pieces*
*60 g/2 oz/¼ cup butter or margarine*
*1 egg, beaten*
*300 g/10 oz/2½ cups plain (all-purpose) flour*
*salt*

*SAUCE:*
*120 ml/4 fl oz/½ cup olive oil*
*2 garlic cloves, chopped very finely*
*1 tbsp chopped fresh oregano*
*1 tbsp chopped fresh basil*
*salt and pepper*

*TO SERVE:*
*freshly grated Parmesan cheese (optional)*
*mixed salad*
*warm ciabatta*

**1** Cook the potatoes in boiling salted water for about 10 minutes or until tender. Drain well.

**2** Press the hot potatoes through a sieve (strainer) into a large bowl. Add 1 teaspoon of salt, the butter or margarine, egg and 150 g/5 oz/1¼ cups of the flour. Mix well to bind together.

**3** Turn on to a lightly floured surface and knead, gradually adding the remaining flour, until a smooth, soft, slightly sticky dough is formed.

**4** Flour the hands and roll the dough into 2 cm/¾ inch thick rolls. Cut into 1 cm/½ inch pieces. Press the top of each one with the floured prongs of a fork and spread out on a floured tea towel (dish cloth).

**5** Bring a large saucepan of salted water to a simmer. Add the gnocchi and cook in batches for 2–3 minutes until they rise to the surface.

**6** Remove with a perforated spoon and put in a warmed, greased serving dish. Cover and keep warm.

**7** To make the sauce, put the oil, garlic and seasoning in a saucepan and cook gently, stirring, for 3–4 minutes until the garlic is golden. Remove from the heat and stir in the herbs. Pour over the gnocchi and serve immediately, sprinkled with Parmesan, if liked, and accompanied by salad and warm ciabatta.

STEP 2

STEP 3

STEP 4

STEP 5

STEP 1

STEP 3

STEP 5

STEP 6

# MUSHROOM & NUT CRUMBLE

*A filling, tasty dish that is ideal for a warming family supper. The crunchy topping is flavoured with three different types of nuts.*

SERVES 6

350 g/12 oz open-cup mushrooms, sliced
350 g/12 oz chestnut mushrooms, sliced
400 ml/14 fl oz/1¾ cups Fresh Vegetable
  Stock (see page 76)
60 g/2 oz/¼ cup butter or margarine
1 large onion, chopped finely
1 garlic clove, crushed
60 g/2 oz/½ cup plain (all-purpose) flour
4 tbsp double (heavy) cream
2 tbsp chopped fresh parsley
salt and pepper
fresh herbs to garnish

CRUMBLE TOPPING:
90 g/3 oz/¾ cup medium oatmeal
90 g/3 oz/¾ cup wholemeal (whole wheat)
  plain (all-purpose) flour
30 g/1 oz/¼ cup ground almonds
30 g/1 oz/¼ cup finely chopped walnuts
60 g/2 oz/½ cup finely chopped unsalted
  shelled pistachio nuts
1 tsp dried thyme
90 g/3 oz/⅓ cup butter or margarine,
  softened
1 tbsp fennel seeds

**1** Put the mushrooms and stock in a large saucepan, bring to the boil, cover and simmer for 15 minutes until tender. Drain, reserving the stock.

**2** In another saucepan, melt the butter or margarine, and gently fry the onion and garlic for 2–3 minutes until just softened but not browned. Stir in the flour and cook for 1 minute.

**3** Remove from the heat and gradually stir in the reserved mushroom stock. Return to the heat and cook, stirring, until thickened. Stir in the mushrooms, seasoning, cream and parsley and spoon into a shallow ovenproof dish.

**4** To make the topping, mix together the oatmeal, flour, nuts, thyme and plenty of seasoning.

**5** Using a fork, mix in the butter or margarine until the topping resembles coarse breadcrumbs.

**6** Sprinkle the mixture over the mushrooms, sprinkle with fennel seeds and bake in a preheated oven at 190°C/375°F/Gas Mark 5 for 25–30 minutes until golden and crisp. Garnish with herbs and serve.

STEP 1

STEP 3

STEP 4

STEP 5

# COCONUT VEGETABLE CURRY

*A mildly spiced but richly flavoured Indian-style dish full of different textures and flavours. Serve with naan bread to soak up the tasty sauce.*

SERVES 6

1 large aubergine (eggplant), cut into
   2.5 cm/1 inch cubes
2 tbsp salt
2 tbsp vegetable oil
2 garlic cloves, crushed
1 fresh green chilli, deseeded and chopped
   finely
1 tsp grated ginger root
1 onion, finely chopped
2 tsp garam masala
8 cardamom pods
1 tsp ground turmeric
1 tbsp tomato purée (paste)
700 ml/1¼ pints/3 cups Fresh Vegetable
   Stock (see page 76)
1 tbsp lemon juice
250 g/8 oz potatoes, diced
250 g/8 oz small cauliflower florets
250 g/8 oz okra, trimmed
250 g/8 oz frozen peas
150 ml/¼ pint/⅔ cups coconut milk
salt and pepper
flaked coconut to garnish
naan bread to serve

**1** Layer the aubergine (eggplant) in a bowl, sprinkling with salt as you go. Set aside for 30 minutes.

**2** Rinse well under running water to remove all the salt. Drain and pat dry with paper towels. Set aside.

**3** Heat the oil in a large saucepan and gently fry the garlic, chilli, ginger, onion and spices for 4–5 minutes until lightly browned.

**4** Stir in the tomato purée (paste), stock, lemon juice, potatoes and cauliflower and mix well. Bring to the boil, cover and simmer for 15 minutes.

**5** Stir in the aubergine (eggplant), okra, peas and coconut milk. Adjust the seasoning. Return to the boil and continue to simmer, uncovered, for a further 10 minutes until tender. Discard the cardamom pods.

**6** Pile on to a warmed serving platter, garnish with flaked coconut and serve with naan bread.

# CHAPTER TWO

# *Pulses*

Pulses – beans, peas and lentils – are the dried seeds of pod-bearing plants of the *Leguminosae* family and are also known as legumes. Rich in protein, iron, calcium and B vitamins, they are highly nutritious, contain plenty of fibre and are virtually fat-free. With the current emphasis on healthier eating, pulses are a must for the modern diet.

Pulses can be cooked in a variety of ways to produce economical and interesting dishes. Many of the world's oldest and most popular recipes are based on pulses, but here are some new versions to tempt you. Try them in burgers, such as Barbecue Bean Burgers (see page 32), as a Lentil Roast (see page 27) for an alternative Sunday lunch or combined with nuts in Chick-Pea (Garbanzo Bean) & Peanut Balls, served with a tasty Hot Chilli Sauce (see page 22).

Opposite: *A wide selection of pulses on sale in a market in Oaxaca, Mexico. Beans feature in many of the national dishes of Mexico.*

**STEP 2**

**STEP 3**

**STEP 4**

**STEP 5**

# CHICK-PEA (GARBANZO BEAN) & PEANUT BALLS WITH HOT CHILLI SAUCE

*These tasty, nutty morsels are delicious served with a fiery, tangy sauce that counteracts the richness of the peanuts.*

SERVES 4

3 tbsp groundnut oil
1 onion, chopped finely
1 celery stick, chopped
1 tsp dried mixed herbs
250 g/8 oz/2 cups roasted unsalted
   peanuts, ground
175 g/6 oz/1 cup canned chick-peas
   (garbanzo beans), drained and mashed
1 tsp yeast extract
60 g/2 oz/1 cup fresh wholemeal (whole
   wheat) breadcrumbs
1 egg yolk
30 g/1 oz/¼ cup plain (all-purpose) flour
strips of fresh red chilli to garnish

HOT CHILLI SAUCE:
2 tsp groundnut oil
1 large red chilli, deseeded and chopped
   finely
2 spring onions (scallions) chopped finely
2 tbsp red wine vinegar
230 g/7½ oz can chopped tomatoes
2 tbsp tomato purée (paste)
2 tsp caster (superfine) sugar

TO SERVE:
rice
green salad

**1** Heat 1 tablespoon of the oil in a frying pan (skillet) and gently fry the onion and celery for 3–4 minutes until softened but not browned.

**2** Place all the other ingredients, except the remaining oil and the flour, in a mixing bowl and add the onion and celery. Mix well.

**3** Divide the mixture into 12 portions and roll into small balls. Coat with the flour.

**4** Heat the remaining oil in a frying pan (skillet). Add the chick-pea (garbanzo bean) balls and cook over a medium heat for 15 minutes, turning frequently, until cooked through and golden. Drain on paper towels.

**5** Meanwhile, make the hot chilli sauce. Heat the oil in a small frying pan (skillet) and gently fry the chilli and spring onions (scallions) for 2–3 minutes. Sitr in the remaining ingredients and season. Bring to the boil and simmer for 5 minutes. Serve the chick-pea (garbanzo bean) and peanut balls with the hot chilli sauce, rice and a green salad.

# KOFTA KEBABS WITH TABBOULEH

*Traditionally, koftas are made from a spicy meat mixture, but this bean and wheat version, which is served with a Middle Eastern salad, makes a tasty alternative.*

**STEP 3**

**STEP 4**

**STEP 5**

**STEP 5**

SERVES 4

175 g/6 oz/1 cup aduki beans
175 g/6 oz/1 cup bulgur wheat
450 ml/³/₄ pint/scant 2 cups Fresh
    Vegetable Stock (see page 76)
3 tbsp olive oil
1 onion, chopped finely
2 garlic cloves, crushed
1 tsp ground coriander
1 tsp ground cumin
2 tbsp chopped fresh coriander (cilantro)
3 eggs, beaten
125 g/4 oz/1 cup dried wholemeal (whole
    wheat) breadcrumbs
salt and pepper
fresh coriander (cilantro) sprigs to garnish

TABBOULEH:
175 g/6 oz/1 cup bulgur wheat soaked in
    450 ml/³/₄ pint/scant 2 cups boiling
    water for 15 minutes
2 tbsp lemon juice
1 tbsp olive oil
6 tbsp chopped fresh parsley
4 spring onions (scallions), chopped finely
60 g/2 oz cucumber, chopped finely
3 tbsp chopped fresh mint
1 extra-large tomato, chopped finely

TO SERVE:
Tahini Cream (see page 78)

black olives
pitta bread

**1** Cook the aduki beans in boiling water for 40 minutes until tender. Drain, rinse and leave to cool. Cook the bulgur wheat in the stock for 10 minutes until the stock is absorbed. Set aside.

**2** Heat 1 tablespoon of the oil in a frying pan (skillet) and fry the onion, garlic and spices for 4–5 minutes.

**3** Transfer to a bowl with the beans, coriander, seasoning and egg and mash with a potato masher or fork. Mix in the breadcrumbs and bulgur wheat, cover and chill for 1 hour, until firm.

**4** Combine the tabbouleh ingredients. Cover and chill.

**5** With wet hands, mould the kofta mixture into 32 oval shapes. Press on to skewers, brush with oil and grill (broil) for 5–6 minutes until golden. Turn, re-brush, and cook for 5–6 minutes. Drain on paper towels. Garnish and serve with the tabbouleh, tahini cream, black olives and pitta bread.

# LENTIL ROAST

*The perfect dish to serve for an alternative Sunday lunch. Roast vegetables make a succulent accompaniment.*

STEP 1

SERVES 6

*250 g / 8 oz / 1 cup split red lentils*
*500 ml / 16 fl oz / 2 cups Fresh Vegetable Stock (see page 76)*
*1 bay leaf*
*15 g / ¹/₂ oz / 1 tbsp butter or margarine, softened*
*2 tbsp dried wholemeal (whole wheat) breadcrumbs*
*250 g / 8 oz / 2 cups grated Cheddar cheese*
*1 leek, chopped finely*
*125 g / 4 oz button mushrooms, chopped finely*
*90 g / 3 oz / 1¹/₂ cups fresh wholemeal (whole wheat) breadcrumbs*
*2 tbsp chopped fresh parsley*
*1 tbsp lemon juice*
*2 eggs, beaten lightly*
*salt and pepper*
*fresh flat-leaf parsley to garnish*
*mixed roast vegetables to serve*

**1** Put the lentils, stock and bay leaf in a saucepan, bring to the boil, cover and simmer gently for 15–20 minutes until all the liquid is absorbed and the lentils have softened. Discard the bay leaf.

**2** Meanwhile, base-line a 1 kg/2 lb loaf tin (pan) with baking

parchment. Grease with the butter or margarine and sprinkle with the dried breadcrumbs.

**3** Stir the cheese, leek, mushrooms, fresh breadcrumbs and parsley into the lentils.

**4** Bind together with the lemon juice and eggs. Season well and spoon into the prepared loaf tin (pan). Smooth the top and bake in a preheated oven at 190°C / 375°F / Gas Mark 5 for 1 hour until golden.

**5** Loosen the loaf with a palette knife (spatula) and turn on to a warmed serving plate. Garnish with parsley and serve sliced, with roast vegetables.

STEP 2

STEP 3

STEP 4

### VARIATIONS

Chopped onion or spring onions (scallions) would make a suitable substitute for leek. Try using different herbs in the mixture to vary the flavour.

**STEP 2**

**STEP 3**

**STEP 4**

**STEP 5**

# RED BEAN STEW & DUMPLINGS

*There's nothing better on a cold day than a hearty dish topped with dumplings. This recipe is quick and easy to prepare and makes a nutritious one-pot meal.*

SERVES 4

1 tbsp vegetable oil
1 red onion, sliced
2 celery sticks, chopped
900 ml/ 1½ pints/ 3½ cups Fresh Vegetable
   Stock (see page 76)
250 g/ 8 oz carrots, diced
250 g/ 8 oz potatoes, diced
250 g/ 8 oz courgettes (zucchini), diced
4 tomatoes, skinned and chopped
125 g/ 4 oz/ ½ cup split red lentils
425 g/ 14 oz can kidney beans, rinsed and
   drained
1 tsp paprika
salt and pepper

DUMPLINGS:
125 g/ 4 oz/ 1 cup plain (all-purpose) flour
½ tsp salt
2 tsp baking powder
1 tsp paprika
1 tsp dried mixed herbs
30 g/ 1 oz/ 2 tbsp vegetable suet
7 tbsp water
sprigs of fresh flat-leaf parsley to garnish

**1** Heat the oil in a flameproof casserole or a large saucepan and gently fry the onion and celery for 3–4 minutes until just softened.

**2** Pour in the stock and stir in the carrots and potatoes. Bring to the boil, cover and cook for 5 minutes.

**3** Stir in the courgettes (zucchini), tomatoes, lentils, kidney beans, paprika and seasoning. Bring to the boil, cover and cook for 5 minutes.

**4** Meanwhile, make the dumplings. Sift the flour, salt, baking powder and paprika into a bowl. Stir in the herbs and suet. Bind together with the water to form a soft dough. Divide into 8 portions and roll gently to form balls.

**5** Uncover the stew, stir, then add the dumplings, pushing them slightly into the stew. Cover, reduce the heat so the stew simmers and cook for a further 15 minutes until the dumplings have risen and are cooked through. Garnish with flat-leaf parsley and serve immediately.

STEP 1

STEP 2

STEP 3

STEP 4

# MEXICAN CHILLI CORN PIE

*This bake of sweetcorn and kidney beans, flavoured with chilli and fresh coriander (cilantro), has an unusual topping of crispy cheese cornbread.*

SERVES 4

1 tbsp corn oil
2 garlic cloves, crushed
1 red (bell) pepper, deseeded and diced
1 green (bell) pepper, deseeded and diced
1 celery stick, diced
1 tsp hot chilli powder
400 g/14 oz can chopped tomatoes
325 g/11 oz can sweetcorn, drained
215 g/7¹/₂ oz can kidney beans, drained and
    rinsed
2 tbsp chopped fresh coriander (cilantro)
salt and pepper
sprigs of fresh coriander (cilantro) to
    garnish
tomato and avocado salad to serve

TOPPING:
125 g/4 oz/²/₃ cup cornmeal
1 tbsp plain (all-purpose) flour
¹/₂ tsp salt
2 tsp baking powder
1 egg, beaten
90 ml/3¹/₂ fl oz/6 tbsp milk
1 tbsp corn oil
125 g/4 oz/1 cup grated Cheddar cheese

**1** Heat the oil in a large frying pan (skillet) and gently fry the garlic, (bell) peppers and celery for 5–6 minutes until just softened.

**2** Stir in the chilli powder, tomatoes, sweetcorn, beans and seasoning. Bring to the boil and simmer for 10 minutes. Stir in the coriander (cilantro) and spoon into an ovenproof dish.

**3** To make the topping, mix together the cornmeal, flour, salt and baking powder. Make a well in the centre, add the egg, milk and oil and beat until a smooth batter is formed.

**4** Spoon over the (bell) pepper and sweetcorn mixture and sprinkle with the cheese. Bake in a preheated oven at 220°C/425°F/Gas Mark 7 for 25–30 minutes until golden and firm.

**5** Garnish with coriander (cilantro) sprigs and serve immediately with a tomato and avocado salad.

---

### CORNMEAL

Cornmeal is made from sweetcorn. It is pale yellow in colour and has a slightly gritty texture. It is available from healthfood shops, supermarkets and delicatessens.

STEP 2

STEP 3

STEP 4

STEP 6

# BARBECUE BEAN BURGERS

*These tasty patties are ideal for a barbecue in the summer but they are
equally delicious cooked indoors at any time of year.*

SERVES 6

*125 g/4 oz/¹/₃ cup aduki beans*
*125 g/4 oz/¹/₃ cup black-eye beans (peas)*
*6 tbsp vegetable oil*
*1 large onion, chopped finely*
*1 tsp yeast extract*
*125 g/4 oz grated carrot*
*90 g/3 oz/1¹/₂ cups fresh wholemeal (whole
    wheat) breadcrumbs*
*2 tbsp wholemeal (whole wheat) plain (all-
    purpose) flour*
*salt and pepper*

*BARBECUE SAUCE:*
*¹/₂ tsp chilli powder*
*1 tsp celery salt*
*2 tbsp light muscovado sugar*
*2 tbsp red wine vinegar*
*2 tbsp vegetarian Worcestershire sauce*
*3 tbsp tomato purée (paste)*
*dash of Tabasco sauce*

*TO SERVE:*
*6 wholemeal (whole wheat) baps, toasted*
*mixed green salad*
*jacket potato fries*

**1** Place the beans in separate
saucepans, cover with water, bring
to the boil, cover and simmer the aduki
beans for 40 minutes and the black-eye

beans (peas) for 50 minutes, until tender.
Drain and rinse well.

**2** Transfer to a mixing bowl and
lightly mash together with a potato
masher or fork. Set aside.

**3** Heat 1 tablespoon of the oil in a
frying pan (skillet) and gently fry
the onion for 3–4 minutes until softened.
Mix into the beans with the yeast extract,
grated carrot, breadcrumbs and
seasoning. Bind together well.

**4** With wet hands, divide the mixture
into 6 portions and form into
burgers 8 cm/3¹/₂ inches in diameter. Put
the flour on a plate and use to coat the
burgers.

**5** Heat the remaining oil in a large
frying pan (skillet) and cook the
burgers for 3–4 minutes on each side,
turning carefully, until golden and crisp.
Drain on paper towels.

**6** Meanwhile, make the sauce. Mix
all the ingredients together until
well blended. Put the burgers in the
toasted baps and serve with a mixed
green salad, jacket potato fries and a
spoonful of the barbecue sauce.

# CHAPTER THREE

# *Pasta*

Pasta is one of the most popular foods on sale today. It is available in a wide variety of colours and flavours, shapes and sizes, and can be bought fresh or dried. Wholewheat pastas have a chewier texture and are valuable for the additional fibre they contain.

All types of pasta are quick to cook and provide a good basic food that can be dressed up in all kinds of ways. From family favourites such as Three-Cheese Macaroni Bake (see page 46) to quick supper dishes such as Mediterranean Spaghetti (see page 38), pasta combines very well with vegetables, herbs, nuts and cheeses, to provide scores of interesting and tasty meals.

*Opposite: Simple, fresh ingredients, such as well flavoured ripe tomatoes, are all that's needed to make a delicious sauce for pasta.*

STEP 1

STEP 3

STEP 5

STEP 6

# COURGETTE (ZUCCHINI) & AUBERGINE (EGGPLANT) LASAGNE

*This rich, baked pasta dish is packed full of vegetables, tomatoes and Italian Mozzarella cheese.*

SERVES 6

1 kg/ 2 lb aubergines (eggplant)
4 tbsp salt
8 tbsp olive oil
30 g/ 1 oz/ 2 tbsp garlic and herb butter or
  margarine
500 g/ 1 lb courgettes (zucchini), sliced
250 g/ 8 oz/ 2 cups grated Mozzarella cheese
600 ml/ 1 pint/ 2¹/₂ cups passata
6 sheets pre-cooked green lasagne
600 ml/ 1 pint/ 2¹/₂ cups Béchamel Sauce
  (see page 77)
60 g/ 2 oz/ ¹/₂ cup freshly grated Parmesan
  cheese
1 tsp dried oregano
black pepper

**1** Thinly slice the aubergines (eggplant). Layer the slices in a bowl, sprinkling with the salt as you go. Set aside for 30 minutes. Rinse well in cold water and pat dry with paper towels.

**2** Heat 4 tablespoons of the oil in a large frying pan (skillet) until very hot and gently fry half the aubergine (eggplant) slices for 6–7 minutes until lightly golden all over. Drain on paper towels. Repeat with the remaining aubergine slices and oil.

**3** Melt the garlic and herb butter or margarine in the frying pan and fry the courgettes (zucchini) for 5–6 minutes until golden. Drain on paper towels.

**4** Place half the aubergine (eggplant) and courgette (zucchini) slices in a large ovenproof dish. Season with pepper and sprinkle over half the Mozzarella. Spoon over half the passata and top with 3 sheets of lasagne.

**5** Arrange the remaining aubergine (eggplant) and courgette (zucchini) slices on top. Season with pepper and top with the remaining Mozzarella and passata and another layer of lasagne.

**6** Spoon over the béchamel sauce and top with Parmesan and oregano. Put on a baking sheet and bake in a preheated oven at 220°C/425°F/ Gas Mark 7 for 30–35 minutes until golden. Serve.

---

PASSATA

Passata is made from sieved tomatoes and makes an excellent base for sauces. It is available from supermarkets and delicatessens, usually in jars or cartons.

STEP 1

STEP 2

STEP 3

STEP 4

# MEDITERRANEAN SPAGHETTI

*Delicious Mediterranean vegetables, cooked in a rich tomato sauce,
make an ideal topping for nutty wholewheat pasta.*

SERVES 4

2 tbsp olive oil
1 large red onion, chopped
2 garlic cloves, crushed
1 tbsp lemon juice
4 baby aubergines (eggplant), quartered
600 ml/1 pint/2½ cups passata
2 tsp caster (superfine) sugar
2 tbsp tomato purée (paste)
400 g/14 oz can artichoke hearts, drained
   and halved
125 g/4 oz/¾ cup pitted black olives
350 g/12 oz wholewheat dried spaghetti
salt and pepper
sprigs of fresh basil to garnish
olive bread to serve

**1** Heat 1 tablespoon of the oil in a
large frying pan (skillet) and gently
fry the onion, garlic, lemon juice and
aubergines (eggplant) for 4–5 minutes
until lightly browned.

**2** Pour in the passata, season and
add the sugar and tomato purée
(paste). Bring to the boil, reduce the heat
and simmer for 20 minutes.

**3** Gently stir in the artichoke halves
and olives and cook for 5 minutes.

**4** Meanwhile, bring a large saucepan
of lightly salted water to the boil
and cook the spaghetti for 7–8 minutes
until just tender. Drain well, toss in the
remaining olive oil and season.

**5** Pile into a warmed serving bowl
and top with the vegetable sauce.
Garnish with basil sprigs and serve with
olive bread.

### SPAGHETTI

Wholewheat spaghetti adds extra flavour
to this dish but you can use plain
spaghetti if you prefer. You may need to
adjust the cooking time, however, so
check the packet.
   When cooking pasta, always time it
from the moment the water returns to a
rolling boil.

**STEP 1**

**STEP 2**

**STEP 4**

**STEP 6**

# SPRING VEGETABLE & TOFU (BEAN CURD) FUSILLI

*This is a simple, clean-tasting dish of green vegetables, tofu (bean curd) and pasta, lightly tossed in olive oil.*

SERVES 4

250 g/8 oz asparagus
125 g/4 oz mangetout (snow peas)
250 g/8 oz green beans
1 leek
250 g/8 oz shelled small broad (fava) beans
300 g/10 oz dried fusilli
2 tbsp olive oil
30 g/1 oz/2 tbsp butter or margarine
1 garlic clove, crushed
250 g/8 oz tofu (bean curd), cut into
   2.5 cm/1 inch cubes
60 g/2 oz/¹/₃ cup pitted green olives in brine,
   drained
salt and pepper
freshly grated Parmesan cheese to serve
   (optional)

**1** Cut the asparagus into 5 cm/2 inch lengths. Finely slice the mangetout (snow peas) diagonally and slice the green beans into 2.5 cm/1 inch pieces. Finely slice the leek.

**2** Bring a large saucepan of water to the boil and add the asparagus, green beans and broad (fava) beans. Bring back to the boil and cook for 4 minutes until just tender. Drain well and rinse in cold water. Set aside.

**3** Bring a large saucepan of lightly salted water to the boil and cook the fusilli for 8–9 minutes until just tender. Drain well. Toss in 1 tablespoon of the oil and season well.

**4** Meanwhile, in a wok or large frying pan (skillet), heat the remaining oil and the butter or margarine and gently fry the leek, garlic and tofu (bean curd) for 1–2 minutes until the vegetables have just softened.

**5** Stir in the mangetout (snow peas) and cook for a further minute.

**6** Add the boiled vegetables and olives to the pan and heat through for 1 minute. Carefully stir in the pasta and seasoning. Cook for 1 minute and pile into a warmed serving dish. Serve sprinkled with Parmesan cheese, if liked.

---

### WOK

A wok is very handy for amalgamating pasta and sauces as it allows plenty of room for tossing the ingredients.

# TRICOLOUR TIMBALLINI

*An unusual way of serving pasta, these cheesy moulds are excellent
served with a crunchy salad for a light lunch.*

**STEP 1**

**STEP 2**

**STEP 3**

**STEP 4**

SERVES 4

*15 g/¹/₂ oz/1 tbsp butter or margarine,
   softened*
*60 g/2 oz/¹/₂ cup dried white breadcrumbs*
*175 g/6 oz tricolour spaghetti*
*300 ml/¹/₂ pint/1¹/₄ cups Béchamel Sauce
   (see page 77)*
*1 egg yolk*
*125 g/4 oz/1 cup grated Gruyère (Swiss)
   cheese*
*salt and pepper*
*fresh flat-leaf parsley leaves to garnish*

*SAUCE:*
*2 tsp olive oil*
*1 onion, chopped finely*
*1 bay leaf*
*150 ml/¹/₄ pint/²/₃ cup dry white wine*
*150 ml/¹/₄ pint/²/₃ cup creamed tomatoes*
*1 tbsp tomato purée (paste)*

**1** Grease 4 × 180 ml/6 fl oz/³/₄ cup
moulds or ramekins with the butter
or margarine. Evenly coat the insides
with half the breadcrumbs.

**2** Break the spaghetti into 5 cm/
2 inch lengths. Bring a saucepan of
lightly salted water to the boil and cook
the spaghetti for 5–6 minutes until just
tender. Drain well and put in a bowl.

**3** Mix the béchamel sauce, egg yolk,
cheese and seasoning into the
cooked pasta and pack into the moulds.

**4** Sprinkle with the remaining
breadcrumbs and put on a baking
sheet. Bake in a preheated oven at
220°C/425°F/Gas Mark 7 for 20
minutes until golden. Leave to stand for
10 minutes.

**5** Meanwhile, make the sauce. Heat
the oil in a saucepan and gently fry
the onion and bay leaf for 2–3 minutes
until just softened.

**6** Stir in the wine, tomatoes, tomato
purée (paste) and seasoning. Bring
to the boil and simmer for 20 minutes
until thickened. Discard the bay leaf.

**7** Run a palette knife (spatula)
around the inside of the moulds or
ramekins. Turn on to serving plates,
garnish and serve with the tomato sauce.

## QUICK SAUCE

For an extra quick sauce, heat 300 ml/
¹/₂ pint/1¹/₄ cups sugocasa (see page 10)
with ¹/₂ teaspoon mixed dried herbs.

# GREEN GARLIC TAGLIATELLE

*A rich pasta dish for garlic lovers everywhere. It's quick and easy to prepare and full of flavour.*

STEP 1

SERVES 4

2 tbsp walnut oil
1 bunch spring onions (scallions), sliced
2 garlic cloves, sliced thinly
250 g/8 oz mushrooms, sliced
500 g/1 lb fresh green and white tagliatelle
250 g/8 oz frozen chopped leaf spinach, thawed and drained
125 g/4 oz/½ cup full-fat soft cheese with garlic and herbs
4 tbsp single (light) cream
60 g/2 oz/½ cup chopped, unsalted pistachio nuts
2 tbsp shredded fresh basil
salt and pepper
sprigs of fresh basil to garnish
Italian bread to serve

**1** Gently heat the oil in a wok or frying pan (skillet) and fry the spring onions (scallions) and garlic for 1 minute until just softened. Add the mushrooms, stir well, cover and cook gently for 5 minutes until softened.

**2** Meanwhile, bring a large saucepan of lightly salted water to the boil and cook the pasta for 3–5 minutes until just tender. Drain well and return to the saucepan.

**3** Add the spinach to the mushrooms and heat through for 1–2 minutes. Add the cheese and allow to melt slightly. Stir in the cream and continue to heat without allowing to boil.

**4** Pour over the pasta, season and mix well. Heat gently, stirring, for 2–3 minutes.

**5** Pile into a warmed serving bowl and sprinkle over the pistachio nuts and shredded basil. Garnish with basil sprigs and serve with Italian bread.

STEP 2

### NUT OILS

Choose any nut oil for this recipe, but remember to keep the heat low as they are much more delicate than other oils.

STEP 3

### LIGHTER VERSION

For a lighter version, use a low-fat soft cheese with garlic and herbs, and low-fat natural fromage frais instead of cream; remember to keep the heat low or the fromage frais will separate.

STEP 4

45

STEP 1

STEP 2

STEP 3

STEP 4

# THREE-CHEESE MACARONI BAKE

*Based on a traditional family favourite, this pasta bake has plenty of flavour. Serve with a crisp salad for a quick, tasty supper.*

\SERVES 4

*600 ml/1 pint/2¹/₂ cups Béchamel Sauce (see page 77)*
*250 g/8 oz/2 cups macaroni*
*1 egg, beaten*
*125 g/4 oz/1 cup grated mature (sharp) Cheddar cheese*
*1 tbsp wholegrain mustard*
*2 tbsp chopped fresh chives*
*4 tomatoes, sliced*
*125 g/4 oz/1 cup grated Red Leicester cheese*
*60 g/2 oz/¹/₂ cup grated Cotswold cheese (see below)*
*2 tbsp sunflower seeds*
*salt and pepper*
*fresh chives to garnish*

**1** Make the béchamel sauce, put into a bowl and cover with clingfilm (plastic wrap) to prevent a skin forming. Set aside.

**2** Bring a saucepan of lightly salted water to the boil and cook the macaroni for 8–10 minutes until just tender. Drain well and place in an ovenproof dish.

**3** Stir the egg, Cheddar cheese, mustard, chives and seasoning into

the béchamel sauce and spoon over the macaroni, making sure it is well covered. Top with a layer of sliced tomatoes.

**4** Sprinkle over the Red Leicester and Cotswold cheeses and sunflower seeds. Put on a baking sheet and bake in a preheated oven at 190°C/375°F/Gas Mark 5 for 25–30 minutes until bubbling and golden. Garnish with chives and serve immediately.

## COTSWOLD CHEESE

Cotswold cheese is a tasty blend of Double Gloucester, onion and chives. It has a medium-soft creamy texture, is pale orange-yellow in colour and is perfect for melting as a topping.

If you can't find any, this recipe would work just as well with any combination of cheeses, so experiment with whatever is available.

# CHAPTER FOUR

# *Grains & Cereals*

The seeds of cultivated grasses are the most universally important staple food. The range of grains and cereals covers varieties of rice, wheat and buckwheat, corn, barley, rye, oats and millet, as well as their associated products such as flour.

Grains and cereals are cheap foods which are highly nutritious, versatile and filling and form a good base to which other ingredients can be added. Each has its own distinctive flavour and texture, so experiment with less well-known grains like millet in Oriental-Style Millet Pilaff (see page 52) or combine a traditional cereal like semolina with cheese to make Cheesy Semolina Fritters (see page 50).

*Opposite: Japanese women hanging out rice to dry after harvesting.*

**STEP 2**

**STEP 4**

**STEP 5**

**STEP 6**

# CHEESY SEMOLINA FRITTERS WITH APPLE RELISH

*Based on a gnocchi recipe, these delicious fritters are accompanied by a fruity home-made relish.*

SERVES 4

*600 ml/ 1 pint/ 2¹/₂ cups milk*
*1 small onion*
*1 celery stick*
*1 bay leaf*
*2 cloves*
*125 g/4 oz/²/₃ cup semolina*
*125 g/4 oz/1 cup grated mature (sharp)*
*  Cheddar cheese*
*¹/₂ tsp dried mustard powder*
*2 tbsp plain (all-purpose) flour*
*1 egg, beaten*
*60 g/2 oz/¹/₂ cup dried white breadcrumbs*
*6 tbsp vegetable oil*
*salt and pepper*
*celery leaves to garnish*
*coleslaw to serve*

*RELISH:*
*2 celery sticks, chopped*
*2 small dessert (eating) apples, cored and*
*  diced finely*
*90 g/ 3 oz/¹/₂ cup sultanas (golden raisins)*
*90 g/ 3 oz/¹/₂ cup no-need-to-soak dried*
*  apricots, chopped*
*6 tbsp cider vinegar*
*pinch of ground cloves*
*¹/₂ tsp ground cinnamon*

**1** Pour the milk into a saucepan and add the onion, celery, bay leaf and cloves. Bring to the boil, remove from the heat and allow to stand for 15 minutes.

**2** Strain into another saucepan, bring to the boil and sprinkle in the semolina, stirring constantly. Reduce the heat and simmer for 5 minutes until very thick, stirring occasionally to prevent it sticking.

**3** Remove from the heat and beat in the cheese, mustard and seasoning. Place in a greased bowl and allow to cool.

**4** To make the relish, put all the ingredients in a saucepan, bring to the boil, cover and simmer gently for 20 minutes, until tender. Allow to cool.

**5** Put the flour, egg and breadcrumbs on separate plates. Divide the cooled semolina mixture into 8 and press into 6 cm/2¹/₂ inch rounds, flouring the hands if necessary.

**6** Coat lightly in flour, then egg and breadcrumbs. Heat the oil in a large frying pan (skillet) and gently fry the fritters for 3–4 minutes on each side until golden. Drain on paper towels. Garnish with celery leaves and serve with the relish and coleslaw.

**STEP 1**

**STEP 2**

**STEP 3**

**STEP 4**

# ORIENTAL-STYLE MILLET PILAFF

*Millet makes an interesting alternative to rice, which is the more
traditional ingredient of a pilaff. Serve with a crisp salad of
oriental vegetables.*

SERVES 4

*300 g/10 oz/1¹/₂ cups millet grains*
*1 tbsp vegetable oil*
*1 bunch spring onions (scallions), white and*
  *green parts, chopped*
*1 garlic clove, crushed*
*1 tsp grated ginger root*
*1 orange (bell) pepper, deseeded and diced*
*600 ml/1 pint/2¹/₂ cups water*
*1 orange*
*125 g/4 oz/²/₃ cup chopped pitted dates*
*2 tsp sesame oil*
*125 g/4 oz/1 cup roasted cashew nuts*
*2 tbsp pumpkin seeds*
*salt and pepper*
*oriental salad vegetables to serve*

**1** Place the millet in a large saucepan
and put over a medium heat for
4–5 minutes to toast, shaking the pan
occasionally until the grains begin to
crack and pop.

**2** Heat the oil in another saucepan
and gently fry the spring onions
(scallions), garlic, ginger and (bell)
pepper for 2–3 minutes until just
softened but not browned. Add the millet
and pour in the water.

**3** Using a vegetable peeler, pare the
rind from the orange and add the
rind to the pan. Squeeze the juice from
the orange into the pan. Season well.

**4** Bring to the boil, reduce the heat,
cover and cook gently for 20
minutes until all the liquid has been
absorbed. Remove from the heat, stir in
the dates and sesame oil and leave to
stand for 10 minutes.

**5** Discard the orange rind and stir in
the cashew nuts. Pile into a serving
dish, sprinkle with pumpkin seeds
and serve with oriental salad vegetables.

### ORANGES

For extra orange flavour, peel and
segment 2 oranges and stir the segments
into the mixture with the cashew nuts.

# GREEN RICE

*Based on the Mexican dish 'arroz verde', this recipe is perfect for (bell)*
*pepper and chilli lovers. Serve with iced lemonade to quell the fire!*

**STEP 1**

SERVES 4

*2 large green (bell) peppers*
*2 fresh green chillies*
*2 tbsp plus 1 tsp vegetable oil*
*1 large onion, chopped finely*
*1 garlic clove, crushed*
*1 tbsp ground coriander*
*300 g/ 10 oz/ 1½ cups long-grain rice*
*700 ml/ 1¼ pints/ 3 cups Fresh Vegetable*
   *Stock (see page 76)*
*250 g/ 8 oz/ 2 cups frozen peas*
*6 tbsp chopped fresh coriander (cilantro)*
*1 egg, beaten*
*salt and pepper*
*fresh coriander (cilantro) to garnish*

*TO SERVE:*
*tortilla chips*
*lime wedges*

**1** Halve, core and deseed the (bell) peppers. Cut the flesh into small cubes. Deseed and finely chop the chillies.

**2** Heat 2 tablespoons of the oil in a saucepan and gently fry the onion, garlic, (bell) peppers and chillies for 5–6 minutes until softened but not browned.

**3** Stir in the ground coriander, rice, and vegetable stock. Bring to the boil, cover and simmer for 10 minutes. Add the frozen peas, bring back to the boil, cover again and simmer for a further 5 minutes until the rice is tender and the liquid has been absorbed. Remove from the heat and leave to stand, covered, for 10 minutes.

**4** Season well and mix in the fresh coriander (cilantro). Pile into a warmed serving dish and keep warm.

**5** Heat the remaining oil in a small omelette pan, pour in the egg and cook for 1–2 minutes on each side until set. Slide on to a plate, roll up and slice into thin rounds.

**6** Arrange the omelette strips on top of the rice. Garnish with coriander (cilantro) and serve with tortilla chips and lime wedges.

**STEP 2**

**STEP 3**

### CHILLIES

Be careful not to touch your face, particularly your eyes, when preparing chillies as the juice can be an irritant. Wash your hands immediately afterwards or wear rubber gloves.

**STEP 5**

STEP 1

STEP 2

STEP 4

STEP 5

# COUSCOUS ROYALE

*Serve this stunning dish as a centrepiece for a Moroccan-style feast;
a truly memorable meal.*

SERVES 6

3 carrots
3 courgettes (zucchini)
350 g/12 oz pumpkin or squash
1.25 litres/2¼ pints/5 cups Fresh
   Vegetable Stock (see page 76)
2 cinnamon sticks, broken in half
2 tsp ground cumin
1 tsp ground coriander
pinch of saffron strands
2 tbsp olive oil
pared rind and juice of 1 lemon
2 tbsp clear honey
500 g/1 lb/2⅔ cups pre-cooked couscous
60 g/2 oz/¼ cup butter or margarine,
   softened
175 g/6 oz/1 cup large seedless raisins
salt and pepper
fresh coriander (cilantro) to garnish

**1** Cut the carrots and courgettes (zucchini) into 7 cm/3 inch pieces and cut in half lengthways.

**2** Trim the pumpkin or squash and discard the seeds. Peel and cut into pieces the same size as the carrots and courgettes (zucchini).

**3** Put the stock, spices, saffron and carrots in a large saucepan. Bring

to the boil, skim off any scum and add the olive oil. Simmer for 15 minutes.

**4** Add the lemon rind and juice to the pan with the honey, courgettes (zucchini) and pumpkin or squash. Season well. Bring back to the boil and simmer for a further 10 minutes.

**5** Meanwhile, soak the couscous according to the packet instructions. Transfer to a steamer or large sieve (strainer) lined with muslin (cheesecloth) and place over the vegetable pan. Cover and steam as directed. Stir in the butter or margarine.

**6** Pile the couscous on to a warmed serving plate. Drain the vegetables, reserving the stock, lemon rind and cinnamon. Arrange the vegetables on top of the couscous. Put the raisins on top and spoon over 6 tablespoons of the reserved stock. Keep warm.

**7** Return the remaining stock to the heat and boil for 5 minutes to reduce slightly. Discard the lemon rind and cinnamon. Garnish with the coriander (cilantro) and serve with the sauce handed separately.

**STEP 1**

**STEP 2**

**STEP 3**

**STEP 4**

# INDONESIAN HOT RICE SALAD

*Nutty brown rice combines well with peanuts and a sweet and sour mixture of fruit and vegetables in this tangy combination.*

SERVES 4

*300 g/10 oz/1½ cups brown rice*
*425 g/14 oz can pineapple pieces in natural juice, drained*
*1 bunch spring onions (scallions), chopped*
*1 red (bell) pepper, deseeded and chopped*
*125 g/4 oz/2 cups beansprouts*
*90 g/3 oz/¾ cup dry-roasted peanuts*
*125 g/4 oz radishes, sliced thinly*

*DRESSING:*
*2 tbsp crunchy peanut butter*
*1 tbsp groundnut oil*
*2 tbsp light soy sauce*
*2 tbsp white wine vinegar*
*2 tsp clear honey*
*1 tsp chilli powder*
*½ tsp garlic salt*
*pepper*

**1** Place the rice in a saucepan and cover with water. Bring to the boil, cover and simmer for 30 minutes until tender.

**2** Meanwhile, make the dressing. Place all the ingredients in a small bowl and whisk for a few seconds until well combined.

**3** Drain the rice and place in a heatproof bowl. Heat the dressing in a small saucepan for 1 minute and then toss into the rice and mix well.

**4** Working quickly, stir in the pineapple, spring onions (scallions), (bell) pepper, beansprouts and peanuts.

**5** Pile into a warmed serving bowl or dish, arrange the radish slices around the outside and serve immediately.

### SERVING COLD

This salad is equally delicious served cold. Add the dressing to the rice while still warm, but allow the rice to cool before adding the remaining ingredients.

STEP 2

STEP 3

STEP 4

STEP 5

# PESTO RICE WITH GARLIC BREAD

*Try this combination of two types of rice with the richness of pine kernels (nuts), basil, and Parmesan cheese, and accompanied by an irresistible garlic-soaked bread.*

SERVES 4

*300 g/ 10 oz/ 1½ cups mixed long-grain and wild rice*
*sprigs of fresh basil to garnish*
*tomato and orange salad to serve*

PESTO DRESSING:
*15 g/½ oz fresh basil*
*125 g/4 oz/1 cup pine kernels (nuts)*
*2 garlic cloves, crushed*
*90 ml/ 3½ fl oz/ 6 tbsp olive oil*
*60 g/2 oz/½ cup grated Parmesan cheese*
*salt and pepper*

GARLIC BREAD:
*2 small Granary or wholegrain sticks of French bread*
*90 g/ 3 oz/⅓ cup butter or margarine, softened*
*2 garlic cloves, crushed*
*1 tsp dried mixed herbs*

**1** Place the rice in a saucepan and cover with water. Bring to the boil and cook according to the packet instructions. Drain well and keep warm.

**2** Meanwhile, make the pesto dressing. Remove the basil leaves from the stalks and finely chop the leaves. Reserve 30 g/1 oz/¼ cup of the pine kernels (nuts) and finely chop the remainder. Mix with the chopped basil and dressing ingredients. Alternatively, put all the ingredients in a food processor or blender and blend for a few seconds until smooth. Set aside.

**3** To make the garlic bread, slice the bread at 2.5 cm/1 inch intervals, taking care not to slice all the way through. Mix the butter or margarine with the garlic, herbs and seasoning. Spread thickly between each slice.

**4** Wrap the bread in foil and bake in a preheated oven at 200°C/400°F/ Gas Mark 6 for 10–15 minutes.

**5** To serve, toast the reserved pine kernels (nuts) under a preheated medium grill (broiler) for 2–3 minutes until golden. Toss the pesto dressing into the hot rice and pile into a warmed serving dish. Sprinkle with toasted pine kernels (nuts) and garnish with basil sprigs. Serve with the garlic bread and a tomato and orange salad.

# CHAPTER FIVE

# *Pastries & Pancakes*

Popular with so many people, pastry dishes can be served either for simple suppers, such as Green Vegetable Gougère (see page 74) or, like White Nut Filo Parcels (see page 73), for more elaborate, special-occasion meals. If you haven't the time to make your own pastry, most shops sell good fresh and frozen ready-made shortcrust, wholemeal (whole wheat), puff and filo pastries.

Pancakes are known the world over in different forms. Egg and milk-based recipes are well known in Europe and use white, wholemeal (whole wheat) or buckwheat flours, whereas white flour and water-based pancakes are more familiar in India, China and Central America; the tortillas of Mexico, for example, which are used in delicious dishes such as Chilli Tofu (Bean Curd) Enchilladas (see page 68).

*Opposite: Made from a few simple store-cupboard ingredients, pancakes are a convenient, versatile dish that's always popular.*

STEP 2

STEP 3

STEP 6

STEP 7

# MEDITERRANEAN VEGETABLE TART

*A rich tomato pastry base topped with a mouthwatering selection of vegetables and cheese makes a tart that's tasty as well as attractive.*

**SERVES 6**

1 aubergine (eggplant), sliced
2 tbsp salt
4 tbsp olive oil
1 garlic clove, crushed
1 large yellow (bell) pepper, sliced
300 ml/¹/₂ pint/ 1¹/₄ cups ready-made
    tomato pasta sauce
125 g/4 oz/²/₃ cup sun-dried tomatoes in oil,
    drained and halved if necessary
175 g/6 oz Mozzarella cheese, drained and
    sliced thinly

*PASTRY:*
250 g/8 oz/2 cups plain (all-purpose) flour
pinch of celery salt
125 g/4 oz/¹/₂ cup butter or margarine
2 tbsp tomato purée (paste)
2–3 tbsp milk

**1** To make the pastry, sift the flour and celery salt into a bowl and rub in the butter or margarine until the mixture resembles breadcrumbs.

**2** Mix together the tomato purée (paste) and milk and stir into the mixture to form a firm dough. Knead gently on a lightly floured surface until smooth. Wrap and chill for 30 minutes.

**3** Grease a 28 cm/11 inch loose-bottomed flan tin. Roll out the pastry on a lightly floured surface and use to line the tin. Trim and prick all over with a fork. Chill for 30 minutes.

**4** Meanwhile, layer the aubergine (eggplant) in a dish, sprinkling with the salt. Leave for 30 minutes.

**5** Bake the pastry case in a preheated oven at 200°C/400°F/Gas Mark 6 for 20–25 minutes until cooked and lightly golden. Set aside. Increase the oven temperature to 230°C/450°F/Gas Mark 8.

**6** Rinse the aubergine (eggplant) and pat dry. Heat 3 tablespoons of the oil in a frying pan (skillet) and gently fry the garlic, aubergine (eggplant) and (bell) pepper for 5–6 minutes until just softened. Drain on paper towels.

**7** Spread the pastry case with pasta sauce and arrange the cooked vegetables, sun-dried tomatoes and Mozzarella on top. Brush with the remaining oil and bake for 5 minutes until the cheese is just melting. Serve.

STEP 2

STEP 5

STEP 6

STEP 7

# SPINACH PANCAKE LAYER

*Nutty-tasting buckwheat pancakes are combined with a cheesy spinach mixture and baked with a crispy topping.*

SERVES 4

*125 g/4 oz/1 cup buckwheat flour*
*1 egg, beaten*
*1 tbsp walnut oil*
*300 ml/¹/₂ pint/1¹/₄ cups milk*
*2 tsp vegetable oil*

*FILLING:*
*1 kg/2 lb young spinach leaves*
*2 tbsp water*
*2 tsp walnut oil*
*1 bunch spring onions (scallions), white and*
   *green parts, chopped*
*1 egg, beaten*
*1 egg yolk*
*250 g/8 oz/1 cup cottage cheese*
*¹/₂ tsp grated nutmeg*
*30 g/1 oz/¹/₄ cup grated Cheddar cheese*
*30 g/1 oz/¹/₄ cup walnut pieces*
*salt and pepper*

**1** Sift the flour into a bowl and add any husks that remain behind in the sieve (strainer).

**2** Make a well in the centre and add the egg and walnut oil. Gradually whisk in the milk to make a smooth batter. Leave to stand for 30 minutes.

**3** To make the filling, wash the spinach and pack into a saucepan with the water. Cover tightly and cook on a high heat for 5–6 minutes until soft.

**4** Drain well and leave to cool. Gently fry the spring onions (scallions) in the walnut oil for 2–3 minutes until just soft. Drain on paper towels. Set aside.

**5** Whisk the batter. Brush a small crêpe pan with oil, heat until hot and pour in enough batter to lightly cover the base. Cook for 1–2 minutes until set, turn and cook for 1 minute until golden. Turn on to a warmed plate. Repeat to make 8–10 pancakes, layering them with baking parchment.

**6** Chop the spinach and dry with paper towels. Mix with the spring onions (scallions), egg, egg yolk, cottage cheese, nutmeg and seasoning.

**7** Layer the pancakes and spinach mixture on a baking sheet lined with baking parchment, finishing with a pancake. Sprinkle with Cheddar cheese and bake in a preheated oven at 190°C/375°F/Gas Mark 5 for 20–25 minutes until firm and golden. Sprinkle with walnuts and serve.

STEP 1

STEP 4

STEP 5

STEP 6

# CHILLI TOFU (BEAN CURD) ENCHILLADAS

*A tasty Mexican-style dish with a melt-in-the-mouth combination of tofu (bean curd) and avocado served with a tangy tomato sauce.*

SERVES 4

1/2 tsp chilli powder
1 tsp paprika
2 tbsp plain (all-purpose) flour
250 g/8 oz tofu (bean curd), cut into 1 cm/
    1/2 inch pieces
2 tbsp vegetable oil
1 onion, chopped finely
1 garlic clove, crushed
1 large red (bell) pepper, deseeded and
    chopped finely
1 large ripe avocado
1 tbsp lime juice
4 tomatoes, peeled, deseeded and chopped
125 g/4 oz/1 cup grated Cheddar cheese
8 soft flour tortillas
150 ml/1/4 pint/2/3 cup soured cream
salt and pepper
fresh coriander (cilantro) sprigs to garnish
pickled green jalapeño chillies, sliced, to
    serve

*SAUCE:*
*900 ml/1 1/2 pints/3 1/2 cups sugocasa (see
    page 10)*
*3 tbsp chopped fresh parsley*
*3 tbsp chopped fresh coriander (cilantro)*

**1** Mix the chilli powder, paprika, flour and seasoning on a plate and coat the tofu (bean curd) pieces.

**2** Heat the oil in a frying pan (skillet) and gently fry the tofu (bean curd) for 3–4 minutes until golden. Remove with a perforated spoon, drain on paper towels and set aside.

**3** Add the onion, garlic and (bell) pepper to the oil and gently fry for 2–3 minutes until just softened. Drain and set aside.

**4** Halve the avocado, peel and remove the stone (pit). Slice lengthways, put in a bowl with the lime juice and toss to coat.

**5** Add the tofu (bean curd) and onion mixture and gently mix in the tomatoes and half the cheese. Spoon the filling down the centre of each tortilla, top with soured cream and roll up. Put in a shallow ovenproof dish.

**6** To make the sauce, mix together all the ingredients. Spoon over the tortillas, sprinkle with the remaining cheese and bake in a preheated oven at 190°C/375°F/Gas Mark 5 for 25 minutes until golden and bubbling. Garnish with coriander (cilantro) and serve with jalapeño chillies.

STEP 2

STEP 3

STEP 4

STEP 6

# CREAMY MUSHROOM VOL-AU-VENT

*A simple mixture of creamy, tender mushrooms filling a crisp, rich pastry case, this dish will make an impression at any dinner party.*

SERVES 4

*500 g/1 lb puff pastry, thawed if frozen*
*1 egg, beaten, for glazing*

*FILLING:*
*30 g/1 oz/2 tbsp butter or margarine*
*750 g/1½ lb mixed mushrooms such as*
  *open cup, field, button, chestnut, shiitake,*
  *pied de mouton, sliced*
*90 ml/3½ fl oz/6 tbsp dry white wine*
*4 tbsp double (heavy) cream*
*2 tbsp chopped fresh chervil*
*salt and pepper*
*sprigs of fresh chervil to garnish*

**1** Roll out the pastry on a lightly floured surface to a 20 cm/8 inch square.

**2** Using a sharp knife, mark a square 2.5 cm/1 inch from the pastry edge, cutting halfway through the pastry.

**3** Score the top in a diagonal pattern. Knock up the edges with a kitchen knife and put on a baking sheet. Brush the top with beaten egg, taking care not to let the egg run into the cut. Bake in a preheated oven at 220°C/425°F/Gas Mark 7 for 35 minutes.

**4** Cut out the central square. Discard the soft pastry inside the case, leaving the base intact. Return to the oven, with the square, for 10 minutes.

**5** Meanwhile, make the filling. Melt the butter or margarine in a frying pan (skillet) and stir-fry the mushrooms over a high heat for 3 minutes.

**6** Add the wine and cook for 10 minutes, stirring occasionally, until the mushrooms have softened. Stir in the cream, chervil and seasoning. Pile into the pastry case. Top with the pastry square, garnish and serve.

## MUSHROOMS

Choose mushrooms that smell fresh and fragrant; avoid bruised or brownish ones. Store for 24–36 hours in the refrigerator, in paper bags, as they 'sweat' in plastic.

There's no need to peel mushrooms. Wild mushrooms should be washed carefully, but other cultivated varieties are better simply wiped with paper towels.

# WHITE NUT FILO PARCELS

*These crisp, buttery parcels, filled with nuts and pesto, would make an interesting break with tradition for Sunday lunch, or even as part of your Christmas Day meal.*

STEP 2

SERVES 4

45 g/ 1¹/₂ oz/ 3 tbsp butter or margarine
1 large onion, chopped finely
275 g/ 9 oz/ 2¹/₄ cups mixed white nuts,
   such as pine kernels (nuts), unsalted
   cashew nuts, blanched almonds, unsalted
   peanuts, chopped finely
90 g/ 3 oz/ 1¹/₂ cups fresh white
   breadcrumbs
¹/₂ tsp ground mace
1 egg, beaten
1 egg yolk
3 tbsp pesto sauce
2 tbsp chopped fresh basil
125 g/ 4 oz/ ¹/₂ cup melted butter or
   margarine
16 sheets filo pastry
salt and pepper
fresh basil sprigs to garnish

*TO SERVE:*
cranberry sauce
steamed vegetables

**1** Melt the butter or margarine in a frying pan (skillet) and gently fry the onion for 2–3 minutes until just softened but not browned.

**2** Remove from the heat and stir in the nuts, 60 g/2 oz/1 cup of the breadcrumbs, the mace, seasoning and beaten egg. Set aside.

**3** Place the remaining breadcrumbs in a bowl and stir in the egg yolk, pesto sauce, basil, and 1 tablespoon of the melted butter or margarine. Mix well.

**4** Brush 1 sheet of filo with melted butter or margarine. Fold in half and brush again. Repeat with a second sheet and lay on top of the first one to form a cross.

**5** Divide the nut mixture and pesto mixture into 8 portions each. Put a portion of nut mixture in the centre of the pastry. Top with a portion of the pesto mixture. Fold over the edges, brushing with more butter or margarine, to form a parcel. Brush the top with butter or margarine and transfer to a baking sheet.

**6** Continue with the remaining pastry and fillings to make 8 parcels. Brush with the remaining butter or margarine and bake in a preheated oven at 220°C/425°F/Gas Mark 7 for 15–20 minutes until golden. Garnish with basil sprigs and serve with cranberry sauce and steamed vegetables.

STEP 3

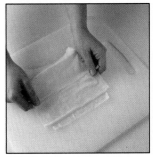

STEP 4

STEP 5

STEP 2

STEP 3

STEP 4

STEP 6

# GREEN VEGETABLE GOUGERE

*A tasty, simple supper dish of choux pastry and crisp green vegetables. The choux pastry ring can be filled with all kinds of vegetables, so try experimenting with your own favourites.*

SERVES 6

150 g/ 5 oz/ 1¼ cups plain (all-purpose) flour
125 g/4 oz/½ cup butter or margarine
300 ml/½ pint/ 1¼ cups water
4 eggs, beaten
90 g/ 3 oz/¾ cup grated Gruyère (Swiss) cheese
1 tbsp milk
salt and pepper

FILLING:
30 g/ 1 oz/ 2 tbsp garlic and herb butter or margarine
2 tsp olive oil
2 leeks, shredded
250 g/ 8 oz green cabbage, shredded finely
125 g/ 4 oz beansprouts
½ tsp grated lime rind
1 tbsp lime juice
celery salt and pepper
lime slices to garnish

**1** Sift the flour on to a piece of baking parchment and set aside. Cut the butter or margarine into dice and put in a saucepan with the water. Heat until the butter has melted.

**2** Bring the butter and water to the boil, then shoot in the flour all at once. Beat until the mixture becomes thick. Remove from the heat and beat until the mixture is glossy and comes away from the sides of the saucepan.

**3** Transfer to a mixing bowl and cool for 10 minutes. Gradually beat in the eggs, a little at a time, making sure they are thoroughly incorporated after each addition. Stir in 60 g/2 oz/½ cup of the cheese and season.

**4** Dampen a baking sheet. Place spoonfuls of the mixture in a 23 cm/9 inch circle on the baking sheet. Brush with milk and sprinkle with the remaining cheese. Bake in a preheated oven at 220°C/425°F/Gas Mark 7 for 30–35 minutes until golden and crisp. Transfer to a warmed serving plate.

**5** Make the filling about 5 minutes before the end of cooking time. Heat the butter or margarine and the oil in a large frying pan (skillet) and stir-fry the leeks and cabbage for 2 minutes.

**6** Add the beansprouts, lime rind and lime juice and cook for 1 minute, stirring. Season and pile into the centre of the cooked pastry ring. Garnish with lime slices and serve.

# THE VEGETARIAN DIET

## FRESH VEGETABLE STOCK

This stock can be kept chilled for up to 3 days or frozen for up to 3 months. Salt is not added when cooking the stock; it is better to season it according to the dish it is to be used in.

MAKES 1.5 LITRES/2½ PINTS/
1½ QUARTS

250 g/8 oz shallots
1 large carrot, diced
1 celery stick, chopped
½ fennel bulb
1 garlic clove
1 bay leaf
a few fresh parsley and tarragon
  sprigs
2 litres/3½ pints/2 quarts water
pepper

1. Put all the ingredients in a large saucepan and bring to the boil.
2. Skim off surface scum with a flat spoon. Reduce to a gentle simmer, partially cover and cook for 45 minutes. Leave to cool.
3. Line a sieve (strainer) with clean muslin (cheesecloth) and put over a large jug or bowl. Pour the stock through the sieve (strainer). Discard the herbs and vegetables. Cover and store in the refrigerator for up to 3 days or freeze in small quantities.

Vegetarianism is becoming increasingly popular in the West. Some people choose not to eat meat because of their feelings about animal cruelty, while others believe that cutting out meat will help reduce the risk of heart disease caused by eating cholesterol-rich foods, and that eating more fibrous vegetables and pulses will help reduce the risk of cancers such as colonic cancer. Whatever your reason for eating meals without meat, providing your meals are properly planned and varied, a vegetarian diet can be as interesting as it is healthy.

## VEGETARIAN NUTRITION

When following a vegetarian diet, your food intake must be carefully thought out in order to ensure the diet is well balanced and provides the body with the correct nourishment. The use of milk, cheese, eggs, pulses and cereals should be maximized to provide sufficient protein, vitamins and minerals. Resist the temptation to eat large amounts of dairy produce in place of meat, however, as cream, butter and cheese contain cholesterol and a lot of fat. As with any diet, keep everything in moderation.

## Proteins

Protein is made up of smaller units, called amino acids, which combine to help the body with growth, repair, maintenance and protection.

There are eight essential amino acids; some foods are better at providing these than others. The main sources of protein

for vegetarians are dairy produce (which contains all the essential amino acids), and nuts and seeds, pulses, cereals and cereal products, each of which is deficient in at least one amino acid. Because of this, two or more of these sources must be eaten at the same meal or combined with dairy produce if they are to be of value to the body.

## Carbohydrates

Used by the body for energy, the two main groups of carbohydrates are starches and sugars, which are present in cereals and grains and related products such as flour. They are also found in fruits, pulses and some vegetables.

**Sugar:** Whether white, brown or in the form of honey, syrup or molasses, sugar is purely a source of energy and has no other nutritional value. Use any type of sugar in moderation and avoid excessive intake.

**Dietary fibre**: Many carbohydrates in their natural, unrefined form, such as wholemeal (whole wheat) flour, contain dietary fibre. It does not have any nutritional value but is vital for the efficient working of the digestive system and the elimination of waste matter. Some types of fibre may also slow down the rate at which the body absorbs carbohydrates. A vegetarian diet is naturally high in fibre. There is no fibre in meat, poultry, fish or dairy produce. Good sources of fibre are pulses, whole grains, vegetables (especially sweetcorn, spinach and baked potatoes) dried fruits and fresh fruits. Try to include at least one high-fibre food per meal.

## Fats

The most concentrated form of energy in the diet and a vital carrier of vitamins A and D. Fat comes in two forms: animal and vegetable. The only animal fats in the vegetarian diet are found in dairy produce and egg yolks.

Fats can be classified as saturated, monounsaturated and polyunsaturated. Saturated fats, such as butter, are solid at room temperature and are believed to raise the quantity of fat and cholesterol in the blood; monounsaturated fats, such as olive oil, are thought to decrease the risk of heart disease and may lower blood pressure; polyunsaturated fats, such as sunflower and corn oils, were at one time believed to be better than mono-unsaturated fats at lowering the amount of cholesterol in the blood, but latest research has found no difference between the two. Polyunsaturated margarines and fats are an exception, however. The oils are made solid by a process called hydrogenation and it is thought that this process can make the fats more harmful than saturated fats. It is important to be aware of this when choosing an alternative to butter. Whatever you choose, keep your intake of fat to a sensible level and cut down wherever possible. Always read nutritional labelling for 'hidden' fats.

## Vitamins and minerals

Vegetables are lower in certain vitamins and minerals than animal products, so it is essential to plan your food intake to obtain the correct nutritional balance.

**Vitamin B group:** Important for the metabolism of other foods, the health of the nervous system and the production of red blood cells. You will obtain a good supply by eating grains, cereals, leafy green vegetables, nuts and seeds and dried fruits. Yeast extract, wheatgerm and brewer's yeast are also good sources.

There are three B vitamins which vegetarians may lack if they consume little or no dairy produce: vitamin B2 (riboflavin), vitamin B3 (nicotinic acid) and vitamin B12. Good sources of vitamins B2 and B3 are mushrooms, sesame seeds, sunflower seeds, almonds, prunes and dried peaches. Vitamin B12 is found mainly in animal products and supplementation is often advised for vegans, as deficiency can lead to anaemia and nerve damage. Yeast extract, alfalfa sprouts, seaweed, textured vegetable proteins and fortified soya milk are other sources of vitamin B12.

**Calcium:** Essential for bone and teeth formation, and for the functioning of nerves and muscles. The best sources are dairy produce and eggs. Vegans and those who don't eat many dairy foods need to eat more grains, pulses, nuts, seeds and dried fruits to obtain a good supply of calcium.

## BECHAMEL SAUCE

This basic white sauce can be use in all kinds of dishes: flavour it with grated cheese or chopped fresh herbs, if you like.

**MAKES 600 ML/1 PINT/2½ CUPS**

*600 ml/1 pint/2½ cups milk*
*4 cloves*
*1 bay leaf*
*pinch of grated nutmeg*
*30 g/1 oz/2 tbsp butter or*
  *margarine*
*30 g/1 oz/¼ cup plain (all-*
  *purpose) flour*
*salt and pepper*

1. Put the milk in a saucepan and add the cloves, bay leaf and nutmeg. Gradually bring to the boil, remove from the heat and leave for 15 minutes.
2. Melt the butter or margarine in another saucepan and stir in the flour to form a roux. Cook, stirring, for 1 minute. Remove from the heat. Strain the milk and gradually blend into the roux.
3. Return to the heat and bring to the boil, stirring, until the sauce thickens. Simmer gently for 2–3 minutes. Season and add any flavourings.

## TAHINI CREAM

Tahini is a paste made from sesame seeds. This nutty flavoured sauce is good served with Kofta Kebabs (see page 24), and other Middle Eastern dishes such as falafel.

*3 tbsp tahini*
*6 tbsp water*
*2 tsp lemon juice*
*1 garlic clove, crushed*
*salt and pepper*

Blend together the tahini and water. Stir in the lemon juice and garlic, season and serve.

**Iron:** Lack of iron can lead to anaemia as it is essential for the production of red blood cells which carry oxygen around the body. Eggs are an excellent source, as are dark green leafy vegetables, broccoli, dried apricots and figs, pulses and nuts. However, as iron from vegetable sources is not readily absorbed by the body it is important to eat foods rich in vitamin C at the same meal as this aids the absorption of iron.

**Zinc:** An important trace element for growth, healing, reproduction and the digestion of protein and carbohydrate. Although wholegrains and pulses contain zinc, a substance called phytic acid inhibits its absorption. Other sources are wheatgerm, oats, nuts and seeds. Useful amounts can be found in most yellow and green vegetables and fruits.

## VEGETARIAN INGREDIENTS

At the heart of any balanced diet is an interesting variety of ingredients.

### Nuts and seeds

Nuts and seeds provide valuable quantities of protein, B vitamins, iron and calcium but also have a high fat content. Nuts and seeds are often pressed for their oil or made into pastes and butters. They add a wealth of flavours to dishes as well as adding texture.

### Pulses

High in fibre and protein and low in fat, beans, peas and lentils come in all sizes and colours. They are cheap to buy in their dry form, but most require overnight soaking before boiling. If you are short of time, use canned pulses. Although canned pulses are more expensive, they are ready cooked and ready to use. Choose varieties that are canned in water without added sugar and salt. Always drain canned pulses and rinse well in cold water before use.

### Grains and cereals

Very important components of the vegetarian diet, supplying fibre, carbohydrates, protein, iron, zinc, calcium and B vitamins. Grains and cereals bulk out the diet and add texture.

### Pasta

A high carbohydrate food which, like grains and cereals, forms the basis of the vegetarian diet. Made from white, wholemeal (whole wheat) or rice flour. All types of fresh pasta, and some dried varieties, contain egg.

### Vegetables

These can be categorized into different groups:

**Leaves:** Lettuces, spinach, watercress, chard, vine leaves. Contain calcium, iron and fibre.

**Brassicas:** Cabbage, broccoli, kale, Brussels sprouts, cauliflower, Chinese leaves. Rich in vitamins and minerals.

**Pods and seeds:** Fresh beans, sweetcorn, peas, mangetout (snow peas), okra. Full of fibre and a good source of protein.

**Shoots**: Asparagus, celery, chicory (endive), bamboo, artichoke, fennel. Better known for flavour, texture and shape than nutritional value.
**Bulbs**: Onions, garlic, leeks, shallots. Excellent for flavour.
**Roots**: Celeriac (celery root), carrots, turnips, swede (rutabaga), beetroot, daikon (mooli). Contain iron, calcium and protein. Carrots are also very rich in vitamin A.
**Tubers**: White and sweet potatoes, yams, Jerusalem artichokes. High in carbohydrate, and useful sources of vitamin C, iron and protein.
**'Fruits'**: Tomatoes, avocado, (bell) peppers, chillies, aubergines (eggplants). Rich in vitamin C.
**Cucumbers and squash**: Including courgettes (zucchini), pumpkins and marrow. Very high water content, Contain some fibre.
**Mushrooms**: Rich in vitamins B2 and B3.
**Sea vegetables**: Increasingly popular and very nutritious. Rich in protein, iron, calcium and vitamin B12.

## Fruits

From home-grown varieties such as apples, pears and soft fruits, to the more exotic imports such as lychees, mangoes and pineapples, fruits are a valuable source of vitamin C and fibre as well as specific trace elements: bananas, for example, are an excellent source of magnesium and vitamin B6, and mangoes provide zinc. Dried fruits are higher in fibre and B vitamins and have a richer flavour than fresh fruit. Look out for sun-dried fruits, and those free from sulphur dioxide, which is used to prevent darkening during drying. Sulphur dioxide inhibits the absorption of vitamin B1 in the body. To cut down on its effect, wash dried fruit in warm water, boil for 5 minutes then rinse again.

## Dairy and non-dairy products

Cheeses, eggs, milk, yogurt, creams and tofu (bean curd) are valuable sources of protein, calcium, vitamins A and D and iron. Cheese adds an excellent flavour to many dishes. Many varieties of vegetarian cheeses, which are made from non-animal rennet, are available. If you choose not to eat dairy products, check the nutritional content of non-dairy products such as soya milks and look out for fortified varieties. Tofu (bean curd) is made from soya milk and is available in many forms – firm, soft, dried or smoked. It is low in fat and high in protein. It can be fried or added to casseroles and soups. It has a neutral flavour and absorbs flavours from the foods it is cooked with.

## Herbs and spices

Careful combining of fresh or dried herbs and spices can add zest to any dish: they help stimulate the taste buds and aid digestion. Experiment with different flavours and read the packet if you are uncertain about strength – most show possible uses and suggested quantities. Don't let any one flavour dominate, they should blend to form a perfect balance.

### SALAD DRESSINGS

Salads are the tastiest and most nutritious way to eat many vegetables. This refreshing, chilled dressing and rich, warm one will liven up all kinds of salads and vegetables.

#### Cucumber Dressing

*200 g/7 oz/scant 1 cup natural yogurt*
*5 cm/2 inch piece cucumber, peeled*
*1 tbsp chopped fresh mint leaves*
*1/2 tsp grated lemon rind*
*pinch of caster (superfine) sugar*
*salt and pepper*

Put the ingredients in a blender or food processor and process until smooth. Alternatively, finely chop the cucumber and combine with the other ingredients. Serve chilled.

#### Warm Walnut Dressing

*6 tbsp walnut oil*
*3 tbsp white wine vinegar*
*1 tbsp clear honey*
*1 tsp wholegrain mustard*
*1 garlic clove, sliced*
*salt and pepper*

Put the oil, vinegar, honey, mustard and seasoning in a saucepan and whisk together. Add the garlic and heat very gently for 3 minutes. Remove the garlic slices with a perforated spoon and discard. Pour the dressing over the salad and serve immediately.

# INDEX